AF433332

Original Title: The Art of Silence:
Unleashing Your Creative Potential

Copyright © 2023 Book Fairy Publishing
All rights reserved.

Editors: Jessica Elisabeth Luik
Autor: Annabel Swan
ISBN 978-9916-728-97-0

THE ART OF SILENCE: UNLEASHING YOUR CREATIVE POTENTIAL

ANNABEL SWAN

The Lilt of Listening

In the quiet of the night,
A gentle whisper takes its flight,
The lilt of listening stirs the breeze,
And secrets dance among the trees.

Soft echoes of the stories told,
In ancient tongues and whispers bold,
The lilt of listening weaves its song,
In hearts that seek where they belong.

Amidst the clamor of the day,
A single note will find its way,
The lilt of listening, a subtle guide,
To truths that often love to hide.

So still your heart, and still your mind,
For in the silence, you shall find,
The lilt of listening, a cherished friend,
Whose wisdom's there, till the very end.

The Lyric of Life

The pen takes flight on parchment fair,
Inscribed with ink, a tale to share,
The lyric of life, a melody,
That sings with endless harmony.

Each day a note, a chance to write,
The story of our hearts, so bright,
The lyric of life, our journey's score,
A symphony we can't ignore.

Through joy and sorrow, love and pain,
Our lives entwined, a sweet refrain,
The lyric of life, a song anew,
With every dawn, a chance to view.

And as we dance upon the stage,
Our lives unfold, from age to age,
The lyric of life, forever true,
The music of our souls, imbued.

Introspective Crescendo

Within the depths of my own thought,
A symphony begins to play,
The notes crescendo, climbing high,
As introspection leads the way.

A melody of dreams and fears,
In harmony, they intertwine,
Reflections dance in moonlit beams,
Revealing truths that lie behind.

Each thought a note, a vibrant chord,
The music swells within my soul,
And as I ponder life's great score,
The introspective takes control.

The final verse, a quiet hush,
As thoughts subside and drift away,
Introspective crescendo ends,
But echoes still in memory's sway.

Harmonious Contemplation

In quiet moments, thoughts take flight,
On wings of harmony they soar,
A dance of contemplation's grace,
To realms of peace, forevermore.

A symphony of whispered dreams,
In gentle tones, a soothing balm,
The mind's embrace of quietude,
In harmonious contemplation's calm.

Each note, a thread that weaves throughout,
A tapestry of thoughts and dreams,
Intricate patterns of the soul,
In harmonious reflection's streams.

The final chord, a soft release,
As thoughts return to present's shore,
Harmonious contemplation's gift,
A tranquil peace forevermore.

Serenade of the Heart

A gentle tune begins to play,
From deep within the heart's embrace,
A serenade of love and warmth,
That fills the soul with tender grace.

Each note, a pulse of life's sweet song,
In rhythm with the beating heart,
A dance of passion, joy, and love,
As serenade's sweet tale departs.

The melody, a soothing balm,
That heals the wounds of life's embrace,
A symphony of tender care,
The serenade of love's own face.

And as the final note is sung,
The heart's sweet serenade complete,
The echoes of its loving tune,
Will live in memory's soft retreat.

The Mind's Quiet Ode

In stillness, thoughts begin to flow,
A quiet ode within the mind,
A gentle stream of consciousness,
Through which the soul's own truth may find.

Each verse, a step within the maze,
The labyrinth of thoughts untold,
A journey deep into the self,
The mind's quiet ode begins to unfold.

The chorus, a reflection's call,
As thoughts converge in harmony,
The quiet ode of inner peace,
A testament to life's journey.

And as the final verse is sung,
The mind's quiet ode at last complete,
The echoes of its wisdom's tale,
Will guide the soul in future's seat.

The Bridge of Balance

Upon the bridge of balance, I stand,
Where light and shadows intertwine,
Each step a dance, a graceful swan,
In harmony, both yours and mine.

The sun and moon, they guide our path,
As day and night, they take their turn,
We walk the line, a tightrope's edge,
To find the truth, we yearn to learn.

In whispers soft, the wind does speak,
The secrets of our fragile fate,
With every breath, we grow more strong,
In love and trust, we navigate.

Upon the bridge of balance, find,
The peace that dwells within the heart,
As hand in hand, we cross the void,
Together, never more apart.

Inward Interludes

Inward interludes of silence deep,
Where thoughts and dreams in shadows keep,
A hidden world, a sanctuary,
A place where hearts roam wild and free.

In quiet moments, all alone,
We find the truth that calls us home,
The whispers of our inner voice,
Guiding us to make a choice.

Through darkest night and brightest day,
The inward journey leads the way,
To find the answers long concealed,
In quiet moments, they're revealed.

Inward interludes of stillness sweet,
Where heart and soul in union meet,
A sacred space, a healing balm,
An inner refuge, safe and calm.

The Resonant Realm

In the resonant realm of dreams,
Where nothing truly as it seems,
We wander 'neath the moonlit skies,
To seek the truth that never lies.

Through forests deep and oceans wide,
With love and hope as our guide,
The resonant realm calls us near,
To face our deepest, darkest fears.

With hearts aflame, we forge ahead,
Through paths unknown, by starlight led,
In the resonant realm we find,
The strength and courage to unwind.

Embrace the mysteries of night,
In the resonant realm's sweet light,
For in the shadows of our mind,
A greater truth we're sure to find.

The Dance of Discovery

The dance of discovery begins,
As we take steps towards unknown realms,
With open hearts and curious minds,
We weave our way through mystic helms.

In every beat, the rhythm sways,
The melody of life unfurls,
The dance of discovery, a quest,
To seek the secrets of the world.

With every breath, our spirits soar,
In cosmic waltz, we find our place,
The dance of discovery reveals,
The beauty of the vast embrace.

The final bow, the curtain falls,
The dance of discovery complete,
With wisdom gained and hearts aflame,
The journey's end, in grace we meet.

An Overture of Insight

In the realm of thought and wonder,
A spark ignites the will to ponder,
Through depths unseen and skies uncharted,
The overture of insight started.

A journey through the mind's own maze,
With every twist, a new pathway,
Unraveling secrets, lost and found,
As wisdom's whispers echo 'round.

Each step reveals a hidden truth,
A tapestry of age and youth,
The strings of knowledge gently plucked,
As insight's song is now conducted.

In the quiet of the final bow,
The melody of wisdom, how,
It lingers sweetly in the air,
An overture of insight, rare.

The Choir of Consciousness

A chorus sings within our souls,
A melody that ebbs and flows,
The choir of consciousness, it calls,
Each voice unique, yet one and all.

In harmony, they rise and fall,
A symphony of dreams and goals,
From quiet whispers to resounding brawls,
The choir of consciousness enthralls.

Each note, a choice, a chance, a plea,
The song of life, a grand decree,
In tune with love and hope, they soar,
The choir of consciousness, forevermore.

And as the final chord is played,
The echoes of their voices fade,
A lasting imprint, memories made,
The choir of consciousness, a serenade.

Notes of Intuition

From deep within, a song emerges,
A symphony of hidden urges,
The notes of intuition play,
A guiding light through night and day.

In every heart, the music thrives,
A silent dance, where truth resides,
A voiceless whisper, soft and wise,
The notes of intuition rise.

Each note, a moment to embrace,
A fleeting glimpse of time and space,
A melody that weaves and sways,
As intuition guides our ways.

And when the final note is sung,
The echoes of the tune still hum,
A gentle reminder of the song,
The notes of intuition, ever strong.

The Ballad of Balance

Upon the tightrope of our lives,
We dance and sway, we strive and thrive,
The ballad of balance softly plays,
A harmony of work and grace.

With every step, a choice is made,
To sway or falter, stand or fade,
The balance found in every stride,
A testament to strength inside.

In equal measure, joy and pain,
The give and take, the loss and gain,
In harmony, they intertwine,
The ballad of balance, a true lifeline.

And as the dance comes to an end,
The song remains, a trusted friend,
A reminder of the path we've walked,
The ballad of balance, forever talked.

Thoughtful Resonance

In quiet moments, thoughts do dance,
A symphony of mind's romance,
Each note played in softest hue,
Thoughtful resonance whispers through.

A melody of dreams so vast,
In shadows of the memories cast,
The heartstrings pluck a tune so fine,
In endless echo, yours and mine.

The soul's crescendo, sweet and pure,
In life's grand opus, we endure,
Through fleeting thoughts, our love's refrain,
A timeless bond, forever sustain.

In twilight's glow, as night descends,
The thoughtful resonance transcends,
And as the final chords do fade,
The beauty of our love's displayed.

Soundless Harmonies

In silence, soundless harmonies,
A dance of whispers in the breeze,
Invisible, yet we can feel,
The tender touch, so soft, surreal.

A symphony of quiet grace,
In every breath, a sweet embrace,
No need for words, the heart can hear,
The soundless music, drawing near.

Through wind and leaves, the song is spun,
The lyrics of the stars and sun,
In quiet moments, we unite,
Adrift in soundless harmonies' light.

Our souls entwined in quiet song,
Through love's refrain, we do belong,
The melody of life we share,
In soundless harmonies, we care.

The Unheard Orchestra

An unheard orchestra does play,
In colors of the night and day,
The music of the world around,
In every sight, yet not a sound.

In vibrant hues, the notes do soar,
The beauty of the world's encore,
Through sunlight's rays and moonlit beams,
The unheard symphony of dreams.

The dance of clouds across the sky,
The song of birds in morning's light,
The rhythm of the earth and sea,
The unheard orchestra's melody.

In every breath, our hearts align,
The world's sweet song, forever mine,
Together in the symphony,
The unheard orchestra, you and me.

Soothing Soul Sonnets

In whispers of the wind, we find,
The soothing soul sonnets entwined,
The gentle touch of words unsaid,
The poetry of love's sweet thread.

Each verse, a heartbeat soft and slow,
The tender warmth of love's sweet glow,
In every line, our spirits sing,
The sonnets of our soul's deep spring.

From depths of love, the words do rise,
The soothing soul sonnets, our prize,
In heart's embrace, the verses penned,
The sacred bond, our souls transcend.

In quiet moments, love is spun,
The soothing soul sonnets, begun,
Through whispers of the wind, we share,
The beauty of our love's sweet care.

Meditative Melodies

In quietude, the heart does sing,
A gentle hum, a calming ring.
Nature whispers secrets old,
Meditative melodies unfold.

The rustling leaves, a symphony,
A chorus sung by wind and tree.
In solitude, the soul takes flight,
Embracing darkness, finding light.

A stillness washes over me,
In meditative harmony.
My thoughts, like birds, do softly glide,
In this serene and tranquil tide.

Suspended in eternal grace,
The world dissolves, all time replaced.
A peaceful moment, sweet and hushed,
Meditative melodies, untouched.

Inward Rhythms

In gentle beats, my heart does play,
Inward rhythms guide my way.
The ebb and flow of life's great tide,
In this dance, I find my stride.

A pulse that travels deep within,
A sacred song, a quiet hymn.
In every breath, a chance to grow,
The rhythm's beat, a steady flow.

In shadows cast, I find my light,
The inward rhythms of the night.
A silent call, a whispered plea,
To journey deep inside of me.

An unseen path, a secret door,
The inward rhythms I explore.
In sacred space, my soul ignites,
The rhythm's dance, my heart delights.

A Dance of Reflection

Through mirrored pools, I softly tread,
A dance of reflection, thoughts unsaid.
The water's surface, smooth and clear,
A canvas for my hopes and fears.

With every step, a ripple forms,
The dance of life in endless storms.
Yet, in this dance, I see the truth,
The beauty of my fleeting youth.

A moment passed, a memory,
The dance of reflection, wild and free.
Through trials and tears, my heart has grown,
In this dance, my strength is shown.

As twilight falls, the dance begins,
The night's embrace, a soothing hymn.
The dance of reflection carries on,
Until the breaking of the dawn.

The Song of Silence

In the quiet of the night,
The stars above, a guiding light.
The song of silence fills the air,
A tender lullaby, a soothing prayer.

The world at rest, a peaceful scene,
A moment's pause in life's routine.
The whispers of a gentle breeze,
The song of silence, hearts to please.

In stillness deep, I find my peace,
The song of silence, sweet release.
The quiet calm, a balm to mend,
The weary soul, the broken bend.

And as the dawn begins to break,
The song of silence softly fades.
Yet in my heart, the melody,
The song of silence, stays with me.

Vibrations of Vigilance

In shadows cast, with eyes alert,
A vigilance that won't avert,
Each subtle sound and whispered word,
Silent wings of a watchful bird.

Through darkest night and brightest day,
The vigilant will never sway,
Their hearts and minds forever strong,
In the quest to right the wrong.

A quiet strength, a steady hand,
With courage, they will make their stand,
Unwavering in their solemn task,
No hesitation when they're asked.

In the pursuit of truth and light,
The vigilant, they stand and fight,
Their spirits joined, their purpose one,
Until the battle's truly won.

The Tone of Truth

The tone of truth, a ringing sound,
In every heart, it can be found,
A beacon shining in the night,
Guiding all to seek the light.

Amidst the lies, it will prevail,
A steadfast ship with sturdy sail,
It cuts through fog and murky seas,
A compass for the lost and free.

Though whispers may attempt to sway,
The tone of truth will never fray,
Its melody, both clear and pure,
A song that will forever endure.

And in the end, the truth will rise,
A symphony of honest cries,
With every note, a promise made,
The tone of truth will never fade.

Sonnets of Serenity

The sonnets of serenity,
A balm to calm the restless sea,
In every word, a soothing touch,
The solace that we need so much.

When chaos reigns and hearts are torn,
The sonnets sing of peace reborn,
Their gentle rhythm, like a breeze,
Brings harmony to hearts at ease.

In quiet moments, they are found,
A refuge from the world's harsh sound,
A sanctuary for the soul,
Where healing words can make us whole.

Through the sonnets of serenity,
We glimpse a world of tranquility,
A haven where our spirits rest,
Embraced within the poet's chest.

The Measure of Mindfulness

In the measure of mindfulness,
We find the path to peacefulness,
A journey through the here and now,
A practice that will show us how.

To be present in each breath,
To find the calm amidst the stress,
In every step, a mindful dance,
A chance to give our hearts a glance.

With every thought, we gently guide,
Our minds to be by our side,
To listen well and understand,
The wisdom of the present's hand.

The measure of mindfulness we seek,
A treasure for the strong and meek,
In its embrace, we find our way,
To a life of peace, come what may.